Moby Dick

Herman Melville

Abridged and adapted by S. D. Jones

Illustrated by James McConnell

A PACEMAKER CLASSIC

FEARON/JANUS
Belmont, California

Simon & Schuster Supplementary Education Group

Other Pacemaker Classics

The Adventures of Huckleberry Finn
The Adventures of Tom Sawyer
A Christmas Carol
Crime and Punishment
The Deerslayer
Dr. Jekyll and Mr. Hyde
Ethan Frome
Frankenstein
Great Expectations
Jane Eyre
The Jungle Book
The Last of the Mohicans
The Moonstone
The Red Badge of Courage
Robinson Crusoe
The Scarlet Letter
A Tale of Two Cities
The Three Musketeers
The Time Machine
Treasure Island
20,000 Leagues Under the Sea
Two Years Before the Mast
Wuthering Heights

Library of Congress Catalog Card Number: 90–82221

ISBN 0–8224–9350–0

Printed in the United States of America

1.98765432

Contents

1 The Spouter Inn

Call me Ishmael. Some years ago I set out to sea. I do this from time to time. Somehow I start to feel like a prisoner on the land. Then I get depressed. I always have to go back to explore the wide open sea. That makes me feel better.

Life began in the sea. So it's no surprise that people long to return to it. It's a place of magic.

When I go to sea, I don't go as a passenger. I go as a simple sailor. Why should I pay when I can get paid for my work?

I don't mind taking orders from some old ship's mate. If I have to sweep the decks or mend a sail, so what? It's honest work. The good Lord thinks no less of me!

The men you find at sea are both good and bad. But I'm always on good terms with them. It's wise to be friendly with the people you spend your days with.

Mostly I go to sea because I want to see the whale. Such a noble creature! And I want to be with those who hunt the whale.

*   *   *

I stuffed a shirt or two into an old bag and left the comforts of home for the Port of New Bedford. I knew little about the town. I didn't know where to stay. Some places cost too much. So I kept looking. I walked up and down the cold, dark streets. The town was like a tomb.

Finally, I saw a dim light near the docks. There was a sign swinging in the cold night air. The sign read: "The Spouter Inn—Peter Coffin."

I shuddered. Coffin? A fine name for an innkeeper. Still, it was a cold night. I had nowhere else to go.

The inn stood on a dark corner. It was a strange and eerie place. It was leaning toward the water. It looked like a sinking ship.

Oh, well, I thought, stop your blubbering. You're going a-whaling soon. There's a tougher life than this waiting for you. So I entered the Spouter Inn.

The inn was a small, cramped place. The wind howled as it whipped through the old house. It was as dark as a graveyard. The first thing I saw was a painting. It was almost black from years of dirt.

Then I took a closer look. I saw that it was a picture of a ship in a great storm. The ship was in trouble. Its three masts were stripped bare by the wind. And a giant whale was leaping out of the water. It was trying to destroy the ship.

The other sailors in the room seemed to care little about the painting. They sat here and there at little

tables. Some drank and sang songs. Others rested.

All I wanted was a good night's sleep. I found the landlord, Peter Coffin, and asked him for a room.

"Sorry," he said. "Nothing left. Every bed is taken." Then he stopped himself and said, "But wait. You don't mind sharing a blanket with a harpooner, do you?"

"Well," I started to object.

"If you're goin a-whalin', you'd better get used to that sort of thing," he told me.

"I guess there's no sense in wandering around anymore tonight," I said. "I'll share the blanket of any decent man."

"Good," the landlord said. "You want supper? Just take a seat. It'll be ready soon."

So I did just that and waited for supper. The place was colder than Iceland. There was no fire, no heat. Just a few candles. The landlord said he couldn't afford the wood.

I ate my dinner with the other men. I saw no sign of the harpooner I was to spend the night with.

I wasn't looking forward to meeting him. No man likes to sleep two to a bed. Most even hate to sleep with their own brothers!

"What kind of a chap is this harpooner?" I asked the landlord. "Does he always keep such late hours?"

"No," said Coffin. "But tonight he's trying to sell his head."

"What?!" I asked. "Sell his head?"

The landlord chuckled. So did the other sailors. Someone was trying to make a fool out of me. Sell his own head! I'm no green sailor.

"Bah," I grunted. I'd had enough bad food and bad jokes for one night. And I was tired of waiting for this harpooner.

I went up to bed. The harpooner's room was cold and dark—like everything else in this old town!

The room was filled with the man's things. A huge harpoon stood over the bed. Beside the bed was an old seaman's bag, fish hooks and . . .

4

What strange thing was this? I saw a kind of doll carved out of wood. But not a doll for little girls. This was an evil-looking thing. Like an idol. Who *was* this harpooner?

I got into bed and tried to get some sleep. But what a mattress! It must have been filled with broken dinner plates!

Soon I heard the door open. I looked up and saw a huge figure. In one hand he carried a candle. In the other hand, he carried—a head!

So *that* was what the landlord and the others were laughing about! The harpooner was selling a shrunken head he'd picked up at sea. Or was it the head of an old bunkmate? I shivered at the thought.

Then the light of the candle lit up the harpooner's face. I started. He jumped.

"Who are you?" he asked.

Lord save me. I had never seen anything like this fellow. His skin was a purplish yellow. And his face was tattooed over with bizarre markings. Was I bunking with a cannibal?

He didn't wait for my answer but instead got undressed and moved over to the black doll. I saw that his whole body was covered with these tattoos. And now he was saying some sort of prayer to the doll. He lit a fire made of wood scraps.

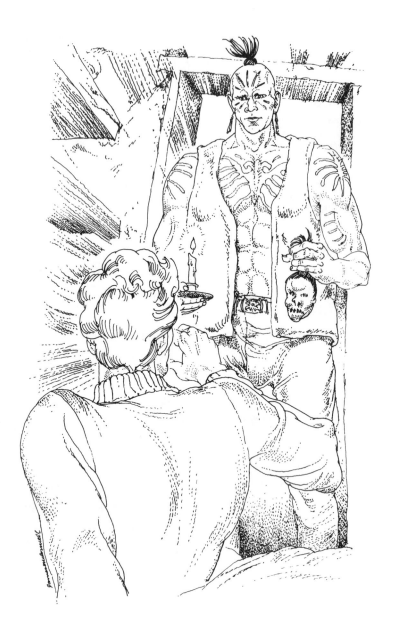

The fire, though small, lit up his strange face. It sent shivers down my spine. As the fire died, he quietly turned from his idol and came to bed.

"I'm Ishmael," I told the heathen. "The landlord said I could bunk with you."

"You no speak," he growled. "Me tired. We get some rest."

"At least tell me your name," I demanded.

"Queequeg," he said simply and turned toward the wall.

Queequeg? It was no Christian name. Still, he seemed quiet enough. Besides, he didn't know anything about *me* either. He could have made a fuss but didn't.

I had no cause to fear, I thought. Better to sleep with a sober cannibal than a drunken Christian. I turned over and closed my eyes. Funny thing. I never slept better in my life.

2 A Close Friend

The next morning I awoke to a scraping sound. Queequeg was shaving. But he was not using a razor. He was shaving with his harpoon. At the time I thought it odd. But after we had been at sea, I knew what fine steel that harpoon was made of.

Though we did not speak much, Queequeg stayed by me. From the moment we opened our eyes, it was as though we were old friends.

We went down to breakfast together. The room was crowded with other whalers. We were all ready to ship out to sea soon. Each of us would choose a ship and off we'd go.

"Grub ho!" cried the landlord, flinging open the door. Soon we were all eating.

Many people think sailors a crude lot, noisy and rough. That's not always so. At least not on land. As I looked around, I thought how quiet this group was. A sailor on land is a strange fish.

I ate my rolls and drank my coffee. But Queequeg didn't care for such food. He only ate beef—rare beef—and plenty of it. Then he sat back and smoked his pipe in silence.

After breakfast I went to church. I didn't think Queequeg—a heathen—would go along. But he never left my side.

There are few sailors who do not visit the Whaleman's Chapel before they set sail. Many of us braved the sleet and snow and walked to the little church.

There we sat, waiting for the pastor. There was nothing to do but read the tablets on the wall. These tablets were memorials to the sailors lost at sea. They all began, "Sacred to the memory of . . ."

Each one went on to describe how some poor fellow—or an entire ship—was lost at sea.

I read one table that still makes me shiver:

SACRED TO MEMORY OF
THE LATE
CAPTAIN EZEKIEL HARDY,
WHO IN THE BOWS OF HIS BOAT WAS KILLED BY
A SPERM WHALE OFF THE COAST OF JAPAN,
AUGUST 3, 1833.

I was about to go hunting and killing whales, and there was a man who was hunted himself and killed by a whale. Yes, Ishmael, I thought, the same fate may be yours.

I was glad to finally see the pastor walk to the pulpit. It was an odd pulpit. Not really a pulpit at all. It was made to look like the bow of a ship. And the pastor climbed up to it on a rope ladder.

His name was Father Mapple. He was well loved by all the whalers. He had been a whaler himself once. But he was old now. Old, but still fit—with a loud, deep voice.

Today, his sermon was about Jonah. Jonah and the whale. He looked down on us and spoke:

"And God prepared a great fish to swallow up Jonah. The book of Jonah is about sin—the sin of not obeying God. But it is also about forgiveness and new life.

"If we obey God, we cannot obey ourselves. Jonah tried to run from God. He hid aboard a ship. But God is everywhere. God found Jonah. Jonah was cast into the sea. He was swallowed by the whale.

"There is an order to the universe. Woe to the man who tries to upset that order. Woe to the man who obeys his own voice but does not obey God's voice, God's heavenly order . . ."

Here again was a story of a whale gobbling up a man. If I hadn't been so set on going to sea, this surely would have scared me off.

But after church, the fears inside me went away. Queequeg and I went back to the Spouter Inn. There we sat before a fire. He sat carving the face of his little black idol. I sat watching him. It was a lazy afternoon.

What a pair we were! The heathen and the Christian. Yet we were closer than I thought. After

all, we were both men, both human beings. And tomorrow we would both choose a ship and set out to sea together. In a way, we may as well have been brothers.

As we sat, I asked Queequeg about himself. At first he just stared at his little idol. He called the doll Yojo. He paid more attention to Yojo than to me. But I kept at him, and finally he answered me.

He told me that he was a native of an island in the South Pacific. His family were members of royalty there. In fact, Queequeg was set to be king of the island one day.

But he did not want to be king. He wanted to join a whaling ship that had visited the island. So one night he left his little island and stowed away on board the whaler. He never looked back.

Queequeg learned many things. He learned to be a great harpooner. He also learned that Christians can be as evil as the people they try to convert.

I looked into his eyes and could tell he was a good person. Even with all those tattoos hiding him. Even with all those heathen markings. You cannot hide the good in a person's soul.

I think Queequeg felt the same about me. For we became a trio that no one could separate—Ishmael, Queequeg, and Yojo, his little black idol.

The next day we awoke with a mission. We would sign on with one of the many ships in port. This was a big choice. We would be on the ship at sea for three years! The voyage could be heaven or hell. It all depended on what choice we made.

Down we went to the docks. Queequeg turned out to be no help at all. It seems his idol doll, Yojo, told him *I* would have to make the choice.

There were three ships to choose from. First I came upon the *Devil-Dam*. Not a good name, I thought. The next was the *Tit-Bit*. I went aboard this one and looked about.

Then I checked out the last ship called the *Pequod*. It was named after an old Indian tribe. As soon as I saw it, I knew that this was the ship for us.

"Look at that ship, Queequeg," I said. "Look at those fittings. It's a weathered old ship. But it's noble just the same. This is our ship."

Queequeg simply nodded and we went aboard to sign up. We met a hard-looking fellow with a great beard. I thought this must surely be the captain.

"Ahoy," I said. "Are you the Captain?"

"No," the gruff old man said. "I be the owner of this ship. What do you want?"

"Me and my friend want to sign on."

"Ever been a-whaling?" he asked.

"No. But I've been to sea many times. And I learn fast."

The owner looked me over and shook his head. "You'll do," he told me.

"Shouldn't I talk with the captain?" I asked.

"That would be Captain Ahab. There's plenty of time to get to know him. You'll know him as soon as you see him. He has but one leg. The other was ripped apart, chewed up, and spit out by the meanest whale that ever lived."

"A whale did that?"

"Aye. And killed many more, they say."

"Is this Ahab a decent man?" I asked.

"Aye. Though some would argue that. He's an unholy, god-like man, Ahab is. Doesn't speak much. But when he does, you'd better listen. You hear me?"

"Yes, sir," I replied. "Now what about my friend?" And I pointed to Queequeg.

The owner looked at him and frowned. "A strange fellow. Marked like a pagan."

"Things aren't always what they seem," I said. "He's a good man."

But nothing I said meant as much as what Queequeg himself did. He took up his harpoon and pointed to a small patch of tar floating on the water. Then he fired the harpoon at it. He hit the tiny dot square.

The owner's mouth dropped. All he could manage to say was, "Quick. Sign him up!"

And so we made our marks in the ship's log. The owner told us to report back to the ship in a few hours.

We were happy seamen, Queequeg and I. I was about to see the world, and Queequeg was going to do what he liked best—hunt.

We walked down the catwalk to the dock without a care. Then . . . we met Elijah. He was a crazy old man who lived down by the piers. He jabbered on about anything to anyone who would listen.

As we walked by him, he grabbed my arm. He asked, "Have you met Captain Ahab yet?"

"No," I said. "What do you know about him?"

"Have you signed on?"

"Yes, yes," I said. "What do you know of this Ahab?"

The old crazy fellow lowered his head and shook it. "Ah, well. What's done is done," he said. "What's signed is signed. No turning back now. But it's a ship doomed, I tell you."

"Doomed?" I laughed. "The old fellow's soft in the head, Queequeg. Be off with you, old man," I said.

But as we passed by him, Elijah turned and softly said, "God have mercy on you."

Bah! I told myself. I was excited about this voyage. And I was not about to let some old fool ruin things for me. Doomed . . . bah!

3 Aboard the *Pequod*

In a few days we would set sail. But there was much work to be done in the meantime. This was no small trip we were taking. We would be sailing for three years!

There were sails to mend, planks to repair, and three years' worth of supplies to stow. The ship carried beef, bread, water, and fuel.

As the gear was being loaded, Queequeg and I often visited the ship. At each visit, I would ask about Captain Ahab. But never did I actually see him. The ship's owner told me he was ill. But he was getting better. He would be ready by the time we set sail.

One quiet morning, Queequeg and I came aboard, and I saw a few sailors moving about the bow of the ship. They went below.

"Look, Queequeg," said I. "Some of the other sailors."

"I see nothing," said Queequeg.

"They just went below. Let's find them. They can't be *shadows*."

We looked below but found nothing. There was only silence. It was as though the sailors had disappeared.

"Ahoy!" I called out, but no one answered. "Those sailors I saw, Queequeg—where could they have gone to?"

But Queequeg was just as confused. They *looked* like shadows. Maybe they *were* shadows.

"Never mind," I told Queequeg. "There's plenty of time to meet our mates."

On Christmas Day, the *Pequod* was dressed and ready to weigh anchor. It was a sharp, cold Christmas. Queequeg and I were on deck, ready to do our captain's bidding. But where was the captain?

We were greeted instead by the first mate. His name was Starbuck. He lined the crew up on deck and bellowed, "Man the capstan! Blood and thunder. Jump, men!"

And so we did. We would always do what Starbuck commanded. He was as brave a man as ever set to sea.

Starbuck was a Quaker and a good, decent man. He was a tall and quiet fellow, thin but strong. Looking into his eyes, you could see all the dangers he must have faced. And his cool manner told you he had faced them all calmly. Yet he was patient when it came to the fear in other men's eyes.

"I will have no man in my boat," he said, "who is *not* afraid of a whale."

Starbuck knew from experience what great damage a whale could do. He did not want any "heroes" in his boat. They tended to be reckless. He only wanted men who were aware of their opponent.

Stubb was the second mate. He was happy-go-lucky. He laughed easily. He laughed at everything—even danger. Even while chasing a whale he would remain calm and cool. He was good-humored, easy-going, and careless. He often sang his seafearing songs in the face of death.

Stubb always smoked a pipe. It never seemed to be far from his lips. In fact, he had a whole row of pipes near his bunk. They were already packed and ready to light.

When he turned in for the night, he would smoke them all. He smoked one right after the other. Then he would fall off to sleep.

The third mate was named Flask. He was a short, stout fellow. He hated whales. He felt that every whale in the sea was out to get him. So he made it a point to get them first. It was a matter of honor for him.

Everyone—Starbuck and Stubb included—meant to hunt and kill whales. But Flask had no respect for whales. He looked upon them as nothing more than big mice. They were pests of the deep. For Flask, the whales were put on the earth only to bother him.

Starbuck, Stubb, and Flask were more than just mates. If Ahab was like a king, these three mates were his knights. Each one would command his own whale boat filled with sailors. Each mate would ride

out to chase the great whales in one of these small boats.

And each mate had his own harpooner. Starbuck chose my friend Queequeg as his personal harpooner. Stubb chose an Indian named Tashtego. Tashtego was strong and dark with long black hair.

Finally, Flask chose a harpooner called Daggoo. Daggoo was a gigantic, coal-black slave. He wore a huge gold hooped earring in each ear. He was a mighty man. He made little Flask look more like a knight on a chess board.

As for the other men who rode the *Pequod*, they were from all over the world. In fact, the *Pequod* was like a smaller version of the world. Men from every country, it seemed, sailed together.

And here we set out on Christmas Day! It was like the birth of a new world. I remember thinking, "What will we make of this voyage? What will become of us in our three-year journey?"

One thing was certain. I was proud to be with these whalers. It's too bad that whalers and whaling have come to be thought of as bad things.

I know that most of you probably think that. Most people think that whalers are no more than butchers. But *you* live on the land. We live on the sea. It's different out here.

Yes, we must butcher the whale. But we do it only to earn our living. We are hated for it. But when soldiers butcher each other on the battlefield, the winners are called heroes. And the women weep over the losers. All of the soldiers are praised! And we whalers are cursed.

Still, the world goes on using the products of our labor without thinking. The oil in your lamps, the candles on your table—even your finest perfumes come from the whale. Remember these things when someone curses the whaler.

For my part, I think that whaling is an honorable profession. It has made me who I am. A whale ship was my Yale College and my Harvard.

And what an education it was! More dangerous and harrowing than any education behind walls. That night we set sail, I would not have traded it for anything in the world.

Soon, we found ourselves upon the wintery ocean. Its freezing spray encased us in ice. A screaming gull flew overhead. The crew looked to the heavens. Each man offered up a silent prayer. We gave three heavy-hearted cheers and blindly plunged into the deep, dark Atlantic.

For several days none of us saw anything of Captain Ahab. Instead, the three mates would take turns on deck.

The owner had told us Ahab was ill but was getting better. Was he really getting better? Or had that strange prophet Elijah been right? Were we doomed?

Then, one day, I came down from my watch. I was tired. I happened to look up and behind me. Shivers ran over me. It was the captain! It was Ahab at last!

4 Ahab's Mission

Captain Ahab did not look as though he had been sick. His whole high, broad body looked as if it were made of solid bronze.

The first thing I noticed was a thin rod-like mark on his face. It was a bright white color. It looked like the mark left in a tree when lightning hits it.

Was it a birthmark? Or had someone or something put it there? I could not say. This mark ran from his forehead, down his check and neck. It finally disappeared under his collar.

There were rumors that the mark had been made during some battle at sea. But had it been a battle with a man—or a whale? Some guessed that the scar went from head to toe.

Ahab cut a grim figure in his black uniform. I was so shaken by his presence that I did not notice the leg at first. One of his legs was missing. In its place was a white peg.

This peg leg was made of ivory. The second mate, Stubb, saw me looking at it. He took me aside.

Stubb said, "The captain had that leg made special. He was at sea near Japan. The ship's carpenter made it from the bone of a sperm whale's jaw."

Ahab placed his peg leg in a hole on the quarterdeck. This kept him steady when the ship rolled and heaved.

Even with this primitive leg, Captain Ahab stood erect. And he looked straight ahead. He never moved his gaze left or right. His stare was fixed and fearless.

He seemed to focus on one thing, one thing only. But what was he looking at? What was he thinking about?

Whatever it was, it must have caused him great pain. The pain showed in his face. It seemed to weigh him down. He was like some great king with kingly problems.

Ahab spoke to no one and no one spoke to him. Not Starbuck, Stubb, or Flask. Nor the sailors. All of us simply went about our business. But we all felt that this captain was somehow troubled.

After a while Ahab went back down to his cabin. But each day after that, we saw him on deck. He would place his white leg in the hole on the deck. Then he stared straight ahead. Sometimes he would sit on a stool or walk heavily to and fro on deck.

As the weather became more pleasant, we saw more and more of Ahab. By and by, winter turned to spring. The harsh icy stare on his face began to melt away. Yet he was still distant and quiet.

We continued to sail farther and farther from home. The ice and the icebergs were now all behind us.

The sun shone brightly. It was spring and the weather was warm. We were sailing in tropical waters now.

The morning air was like perfume. The night sky was deep and clear. The stars shone by the millions. They looked like diamonds set in black velvet.

Our days and nights passed one like the other. It was an easy time. A quiet time. It would never again be this nice.

One of my duties was to sit atop the masthead and watch for whales. On some ships, the lookout is enclosed, like a crow's nest. But we were going to hunt whales in southern waters. So the lookout was open. In bad weather I had nothing but my coat to give me shelter. It was hard to cling to that little seat, I can tell you.

I was on lookout one night. I could see the captain pacing back and forth on the deck. Earlier in our voyage, we had hardly ever seen him. Now, he never seemed to go below. He never seemed to sleep. He paced.

That night, his peg leg was making an awful noise. Though I was on watch, I felt sorry for my mates. I knew it was hard getting rest with that clump-clump going on above.

Soon the second mate, Stubb, came on deck. He looked a little sheepish.

He said, "Captain, I beg your pardon. If you care to walk the deck, sir, no one will say no to you, but, uh . . . would there be some way to muffle the sound? You see, my men are—"

But the captain interrupted him. "Who do you think you're talking to?"

"Sir, I—"

"Never mind. Never mind. I had forgotten. Your men need their sleep. Go below to your nightly grave, dog! Go!"

Stubb did not move. "I am not used to being called such names," he told Ahab. "I must say, sir, that I don't much like it."

"Get below, I said, or I'll rid the world of you," bellowed the captain. And having said that, he made a violent move toward Stubb.

The captain looked as though he would kill Stubb. And Stubb was no small man. But even *he* had to move away. He went below deck.

How Ahab had flashed at him! Was the captain mad? There was something on his mind, I was sure of that.

Though the captain stopped his noisy pacing, he did not go below. He was only in his bunk three hours out of twenty-four.

All of us wondered what made Ahab so angry. We wondered what possessed him so. The next day, we all found out.

I was asleep when I heard first mate Starbuck call, "All hands on deck."

I stumbled my way from my bunk and up on deck. The minute I saw the captain, I knew something was wrong. The little monster that had been locked up inside him was about to work its way out.

Captain Ahab stood before the entire crew. He asked us, "What do you do when ye see a whale, men?"

"Sing out for him," we all said at once.

"Good!" cried Ahab with wild approval in his voice. "And what do you do next, men?"

"Lower away, and go after him," we replied.

He said, "Some of you sailors have never before heard me give orders about a white whale. So watch this."

He reached into his pocket and took out a large, gold coin. It shone brightly. It looked like a small sun sitting right there in the captain's palm.

"Do ye see this Spanish ounce of gold?" Ahab asked. It is a sixteen-dollar piece. Do you see it?"

Then he commanded first mate Starbuck to fetch him a hammer and nail. Starbuck did as he was commanded and returned.

Ahab took the hammer and nail in hand. He rubbed the gold coin against his uniform to polish it. Then he placed the coin upon the mainmast. And with a mighty thrust he hammered the nail through the coin and into the mast. The gold coin stuck in the mast. It glistened in the sun.

Ahab said, "Whoever first spots this white whale shall have the gold coin. This is no ordinary whale.

"Now listen. The beast I seek is a white-headed whale. It has a wrinkled brow and a crooked jaw. Three holes have been made in his right fluke. Remember. It's a white whale I want. White. Look sharp for it. If you see even a bubble of water, sing out. If it be the whale I look for, the gold is yours!"

We all let out a loud cheer. We all stared at that coin. It was a beautiful sight to see.

I looked over at Queequeg. He looked troubled. So did the other harpooners, Tashtego and Daggoo.

"Captain Ahab," said Tashtego. "Is this white whale the same one they call Moby Dick?"

"Moby Dick?" shouted Ahab. "Do you know the white whale then, Tash?"

"Aye. He has a strange way of diving, he does," replied Tashtego.

And Daggoo added, "I know him, too, Captain. He lets loose with a huge, bushy spout of water."

Then Queequeg spoke up. "I seen him, I did. There be many harpoons still stuck and rusted in his flesh. They be all twisted and wrenched in his gut. But he swims on like they was only pins."

For the first time I saw a smile cross Captain Ahab's face. "Aye, men. Aye. Then you've seen him. You've seen Moby Dick! Moby Dick!"

Ahab's smile was not the smile of a little child, pleased with some toy. It was a crazy, wicked smile. And it scared me.

Starbuck had been eying the captain cautiously. He said, "Captain Ahab, I have heard of Moby Dick. Wasn't this the whale that took off your leg?"

The smile on Ahab's face disappeared. "Aye, Starbuck. Aye, shipmates all. It was Moby Dick that crippled me. Moby Dick gave me this dead stump I now stand on. Aye, it was that blasted white whale."

He let out a cry like a wounded animal. It was a sad and sickening cry.

Ahab shouted, "I'll chase him around Good Hope. I'll chase him round the Horn. I'll follow him into the flames of hell before I'll give him up."

Then he turned back to us all. He stared at each one of us. Fire burned in his eyes.

He said, "This is what you have shipped for, men. To chase that white whale through all the oceans on earth. To hunt him down till he spouts black blood and gives up the ghost.

"What say you, men? Are you brave enough to handle the beast? Are you ready? Are you with me?"

"Aye! Aye!" shouted the harpooners and the sailors alike. "We'll keep a sharp eye for Moby Dick. And a sharp harpoon as well," we all said.

"God bless you, men," Ahab said with a sob. Then he commanded Flask to bring us some wine. "We'll drink to it, men," he said. "We'll drink to our pact to rid the waters of this evil beast."

All the men let out a cheer. All but one. Starbuck was as grim as death.

"What's the sad face about, Mr. Starbuck? Will you not chase the white whale? Are you not brave enough?"

Starbuck replied, "I am brave enough to face his crooked jaw. And the jaws of death, too. But I came aboard to hunt all whales. Not just one whale. I did not come aboard to help my captain get back at some dumb beast.

"The whale struck at you out of blind instinct," Starbuck said. "It did not strike you out of some inner evil. Yet you strike back at this brute out of cruelty. That is madness."

"Madness!" cried Ahab. "Listen to me, man. Moby Dick only looks like a dumb brute. Beneath that whale's mask there is an evil power. That is what I hate."

"He is just a whale," said Starbuck.

Ahab replied, "Maybe Moby Dick is only the agent of some evil power. Or maybe he is the evil power himself. But he weighs me down with hate."

"Then you are a sad man."

"Am I? Moby Dick is in my every waking thought. He haunts my dreams. I can see only the white whale.

His presence in the world insults me. And I'd strike the sun itself if it insulted me."

Starbuck could see the captain would no longer listen to him. He turned away and said softly, "God help us. God help us all."

Flask returned with the wine. Ahab took up the wine and held it high. "Each of you! Drink the wine and pass it," he yelled to us.

We did as we were told. The crew wanted to drink. The captain had gotten them fired up. Ahab's mission was now their mission.

"Harpooners!" he cried out. "Bring your lances to me and cross them."

Queequeg, Tashtego, and Daggoo grabbed hold of their harpoons. They crossed them before Ahab. The captain grabbed hold of each of the harpoons.

He said, "Drink, you harpooners. Drink and swear, you men that man the whaleboat's bow. Death to Moby Dick! God hunt us all if we do not hunt Moby Dick to his death!"

Before he went below, Ahab turned back to all of us. "Remember—you have all made a vow," he said. Then he disappeared below deck.

I shuddered at the thought. What a pledge we had made! Captain Ahab was surely mad. He was madness itself. And we had pledged ourselves to his madness.

5 A Stormy Sighting

I, Ishmael, was one of that crew. My shouts had gone up with the rest. My oath was bound together with their oaths. I shouted just as loudly and as strongly as any man on board. Ahab's struggle was now mine as well.

I set about to learn everything I could about Moby Dick. It seemed there was much to learn. Many of the older seamen had stories to tell about the monster of the deep. It was plain, though, that few had ever actually seen him.

Queequeg and I joined some others to listen to the tales. We gathered around one old seaman with a snow-white beard and an ivory pipe.

"Aye. I heard tell of the beast," said the old man. "A murderous fellow he is, too. He's bigger than other sperm whales. As big as this very ship. His skull is white. As white as the first snowfall. And his brow is wrinkled. His jaw is mighty. It be crooked as an old man. But don't let that fool you. It can cut a whaler in half like a matchstick.

"But the worst is still to come," the old man continued. "If ever you go after him, be sure to do it to the death. For when Moby Dick is hunted, he'll turn on the hunters. No harpoon can stop him. He has a treasure of iron in him even now. The harpoon may cut his flesh, but it won't kill him."

The old man looked at us all and nodded. He took a deep puff on his pipe. "I can see that some of you don't believe me. Well, go ask the captain. For it was Ahab himself rode out to kill Moby Dick. Ahab the hunter became the hunted. He took up his steel shaft to plunge into Moby Dick's side.

"Then the whale turned and sawed off the captain's leg at the hip. Snap! And worst still, they say the beast enjoyed the task. Evil runs through its veins, like blood through a human being. That whale is evil itself in the flesh. At least he be so for Ahab."

Such stories were common. I had been listening to these tales for days. One of the wildest I'll tell you now.

Some of the sailors said the whale could be in more than one place at the same time! They said Moby Dick had been spotted in two different oceans—thousands of miles apart—in the same instant.

Others said he could never be killed. I did not believe such tales. But other stories I did believe. For the facts were as frightening as the fables.

It is common for a sperm whale to carry harpoons in its side. Not all harpoons will kill a whale. The sight of all that iron in Moby Dick did not mean that he was beyond killing. But it *did* mean he was stronger than most other whales.

As for Moby Dick's anger? Well, ask any whaler. Any sperm whale is a worthy opponent. He can frighten even the bravest man. Many whalers have been killed by whales. I have even heard of a sperm whale ramming and sinking a Navy ship!

And what about other sea creatures? They, too, fear the sperm whale. Even sharks!

So it did not surprise me that Ahab thought that the white whale was evil. But as for me, I was not so sure.

It was Moby Dick's odd color that Ahab kept talking about. It was white. But why should the color white be evil?

White can mean many things to many people. White can mean good luck. Seeing a white stone brought joy to the ancient Romans. A polar bear is white. And we don't think of a polar bear as evil. We think of him as strong.

In some old stories, white means just the opposite of evil. It means purity. No, I was not so sure that Moby Dick was all evil.

No one thing made by God can have only one meaning. Anything can be looked at in many different ways. It can be seen as evil or good. It just depends on how you choose to see it.

So Moby Dick, too, can be looked at in many different ways. If white can be thought of as good and evil, so could Moby Dick, I thought. But it was obvious to me that Captain Ahab would not agree.

I choose to see both good and evil in people. And I chose to see both the good and the evil in Moby Dick. Ahab, in his madness, chose to see only the evil.

Yet, Ahab knew that he was given another task. A task other than his revenge. He was told to bring back whale oil. And that meant killing whales other than Moby Dick. It might be months before we ever spotted the white whale.

So we were told to keep a sharp eye for any whale. Up to this point, I had never been on a whale hunt. But all that was to change soon.

The days had passed by easily and slowly. One was much like the other. We all had our tasks to do and we did them.

I was mending a sail and listening to stories of Moby Dick. My mind was a thousand miles away. Then I heard a voice. It was Queequeg's.

"There she blows! There! There! She blows!" he cried.

We all looked up. There, a way off, we saw a school of sperm whales. The whole crew went into action. This was the moment I had been waiting for.

Each man knew what he was supposed to do. Still, there was a lot of confusion. The sailors were running all over the ship.

My heart started pounding. I looked once more at the whales. Was any one of them Moby Dick, I wondered? No. I remembered that he always swims alone. I breathed a sigh of relief. I did not want to meet Moby Dick my first time out.

The small boats were swung out over the open sea and lowered. This was it. This was to be the adventure I had wondered about for so long—the whale hunt.

But just as I was about to make my way to the small boat, I saw them. The five shadowy figures I had seen boarding the boat back at home port.

They seemed to come out of nowhere. They seemed to appear from thin air. So I was *not* crazy. I really *had* seen them before. But who were they?

They were not ghosts. I was sure of that now. They were real men. But they must have spent all this time below decks. They were just waiting. But for what?

"Who are they?" I asked Stubb, the second mate.

Stubb said, "They're part of Ahab's special crew." He laughed to himself as he grabbed his gear. "Most captains don't get into the hunt. But Ahab's not like other captains. Those men of his work like a machine."

Soon, the captain's crew had lowered his boat into the water. The captain called out to his men and they were off.

Starbuck, Stubb, and Flask wasted no time in following.

"Avast, you men!" cried Starbuck. "In the boats and away."

I felt suddenly afraid away from the ship. There I was, eye level with the sea. I was in the whale's world now. I was in his territory. I felt odd, strange. How could mere men possibly catch and kill a whale like this?

Off we went. Starbuck, Stubb, and Flask were each calling out to their men. They wanted them to row faster and faster.

I was pulling as hard as I could. But I soon came to realize something. There was great competition between the boats, between the mates.

As fast as we rowed, so swam the whales. They were like arrows shot through the air. They seemed to fly through the water.

"Onward, men!" shouted Starbuck. "Put some muscle into it."

My back and legs started to burn. I was pulling as hard as I could. Why was it so hard? I wondered.

I was so set on being the first to reach the whales I did not notice the rain. A storm had swooped up out of the north. The waves grew bigger.

The sea grew more and more angry. The waves crashed into our small boat with a fury. It became clear that the whales would escape. But the whales were the least of my worry now.

During the chase, our ship, the *Pequod* had followed us. But during the storm the waves had turned the great ship around. Now it was in front of us, directly in our path.

I looked behind me and saw the great hulk of the ship. It was coming right at our boat. It was no more than a hundred yards off and gaining on us fast.

I dipped my oar in the water and pulled as hard as I could. But thank God Starbuck was thinking more clearly than I was.

"Save yourselves, men," he cried. "She's on us!"

All around me the other whalers were diving overboard. They were swimming for their lives.

"Hurry, men!" said Starbuck. He made sure every last man was off the boat before he saved himself.

I dove into the cold waters and swam for all I was worth. I looked up and saw the ship. It was only a few yards off now.

Would I make it? I thought for sure I would be crushed under the *Pequod's* giant hull.

I swam harder and harder. But the waves were fierce. I heard men shouting. There was a terrible crash. I looked up. I had gotten clear of the *Pequod*. But our small boat had been crushed to splinters.

I seemed to be treading water for hours. I was, in fact, the last man to be pulled from the stormy waves.

I fell onto the deck of the *Pequod*. I was safe at last. I coughed a sea full of water from my lungs. Still, I was happy to be alive.

Queequeg was the first to rush to my side. "You all right now," he assured me. "You fine now." He held me in his arms and dried me off.

"Did we lose any men?" I asked, gasping for breath.

"No," said Starbuck. "All are on board now. Safe as babies."

When I finally looked up, I expected to hear moaning and groaning. Men praying to God in thanks. Instead, some of the men were laughing with thanksgiving. Others simply took it in stride. It seemed to mean little to them.

"Is this a very common thing?" I asked Starbuck.

"Aye, that it is," came his reply. "Death is an angel that always hovers over the whaler, my friend."

What an experience on our first sighting! I had almost been killed and never got near a whale!

I saw the others all patting one another on the back. Some were telling their own stories. They said they thought they were dead. They told how they swam to safety.

I soon realized that every time I went out I would be risking my life. If the whales didn't turn on us, the sea might. The sea and the whales were mighty creatures. I was a tiny man.

So I took Queequeg below deck and made out a will. He was my witness. He put his mark to it.

I began to calm down. Soon, I was just like the others. What a cool, calm dive at death we had all made. It had bound us together and made us all like brothers.

6 The First Hunt

After my fears went away, I longed for the next sighting. I had not gotten close to the whales my first time out. I wanted another chance.

But with whaling, I soon found, many days may pass between sightings. Then you might spend the next few days at the hunt.

So Queequeg and I passed the time. We did our chores. We did them without grumbling. But we also had time for fun.

A boy named Pip sang and danced for us. He was a merry little youth. He could make us all sing and laugh and forget our cares.

Other sailors passed the time by "skrimshandering." Don't know what that means, eh? You wouldn't except you went a-whaling. Skrimshandering is carving.

The sailors work at carving in all sorts of things. They use a knife and make scenes in whale bone. Sometimes they use wood and even metal.

The images they make are beautiful. I've seen lots of paintings of whales done by land-loving artists. They aren't very true to life. In my opinion, whalers are the only ones who know how to draw the whale.

Queequeg made some beautiful carvings. But I was never very handy at it. So I just watched him.

The best part of our rest came when we saw other ships. It gets very lonely out at sea. Weeks go by and you don't see another soul. But every now and then you'll meet another ship.

When that happens both captains draw their ships close by. The captain and crew of one ship will always stop and talk with the other. This is called a "gam."

The gam is used as a time of fellowship. "What have you seen?" or "Where have you been?" or "Do you need help?" Such calls are common.

But with Ahab the gams were different. He did not much like gams. They just took away from his time to seek Moby Dick. Moby Dick took up all his thoughts. So he had no time to waste.

The first question Ahab would ask another ship was, "Have you seen the white whale?" Usually, if the reply was "no," he'd cut the gam short.

Ahab wasn't interested in passing the time. He wasn't interested in chit-chat. Ahab was only interested in killing the white whale.

The crew was not happy about that. Most of the sailors longed to see other sailors. But what could we say? We had pledged ourselves to the captain's desires. And all for a piece of gold!

It should be no surprise that the white whale was in all our minds. We thought we saw him everywhere.

43

Even Daggoo, the giant slave, thought he saw Moby Dick.

One day he cried out, "There! He breaches! Right ahead. The white whale!"

All hands scurried to starboard to take a look. But it was nothing more than a giant squid.

"The squid's an evil omen," Flask said bitterly. "It's a devilish beast."

Strange, I thought. The sea can look like such a calm and peaceful place. But look again. All around, one creature feeds on another. Large fish feed on smaller ones. And even the large ones aren't safe. The sea itself can be their enemy. Waves can dash a giant whale against the rocks as if it were a small boat.

The sea gives life and takes it away. It's a place of wonder and terror. And everyone seeks a little island of safety from it. All I can say, my friend, is find that island of peace and safety. And when you do, thank God for it and stay there.

"Just look at that squid," Flask said. "Look at its legs twisting all about like snakes. Aye, when you see a squid, 'tis bad luck."

But Queequeg did not agree. "No," he said firmly. "Where there be squid, there be whales." As usual, Queequeg was right. We soon came upon a huge stretch of yellow ocean.

"What the devil is that?" I asked.

Starbuck was standing beside me and answered, "Tiny creatures. I call them 'brit.' "

"Brit?"

"They're smaller than the point of a pin. But there are millions of them. They turn the sea yellow. The whale feeds on them. And that—my fine sailor—is a *good* omen indeed."

Sure enough, it was. We could see huge patches of blue ocean in between the yellow. That's where the giant whales had passed through. They open their huge jaws and swallow up the yellow stuff.

That patch of brit meant that we were not far behind the whales. I would get my chance at a whale again, sooner than I thought.

It was my turn to stand watch. I had been at my lookout for hours, and I was growing sleepy. Suddenly I saw a gigantic sperm whale.

Could it be Moby Dick? I looked hard. It wasn't white. No, it wasn't Moby Dick. But it was a huge whale, that was certain.

It was lazily drifting in the sea. It too, seemed to be sleepy just like me. The whale reminded me of an old, fat uncle of mine. He used to lie like that big whale, smoking a pipe on a warm afternoon. Poor old whale. This warm, lazy afternoon would be his last.

"There she blows!" I cried. "Not forty fathoms off!"

The crew came to life.

"Clear away the boats," cried Ahab.

The small boats hit the water. I climbed aboard Stubb's boat this time and away we went.

We had a calm day today. No storm in sight. This time, nothing would stop us.

But all our yelling and crying out must have alarmed the whale. He knew he was in trouble. The whale began to swim away fast.

Stubb cheered us on. "There she flukes! Don't hurry yourselves. Take your time. Make it count this time. Stay cool. We're almost on top of him now."

I pulled hard and strong. But this time I was calm.

"NOW!" cried Stubb. "Stand up, Tashtego. Give it to him."

Tashtego hurled his harpoon. It struck the whale. A direct hit!

The harpoon was attached to a rope coiled in the bottom of the boat. The rope started to unwind. It whizzed by us. Good thing the rope was strong enough to bear the strain of three tons. This whale was a big one.

The rope burned as it passed through our hands. It was like holding the blade of a two-edged sword.

Stubb stood and took hold of the line. "Wet the line! Wet the line!" he cried.

We were attached to the whale as it swam. The boat now flew through the water. The whale tried to swim free. We were moving at a fantastic rate.

The whale's wake swirled all around our boat. I thought for sure we would turn over. Each man clung to his position. Tashtego and Stubb grabbed the harpoons.

We brought the whale in closer. Stubb made his first dart—or throw—at the whale. Then another dart and another. The whale slowed, but not by much. We brought the boat closer.

The whale sensed now that its life was over. But by some deep instinct it tried with all its might to survive. It blew huge spouts of spray at us. It tried to race away.

Once again Stubb threw his dart into the whale's side. Again and again. Blood began to shoot from the whale. It covered all of us. I had never seen so much blood in my life. It was a strange and unhappy sight. Such a great and grand life was ending before my eyes.

The whale slowed. The sea around us turned red with the beast's blood. Stubb drew closer to the whale. It was hardly moving now.

Stubb stood atop the whale. He drove his lance deeper and deeper into the whale's side. Finally, it pierced the whale's heart. The giant suddenly shook and thrashed about—and finally died.

All was calm again. The red sea swelled beneath us. Stubb was covered in blood.

I had been on my first *real* hunt, and what a sight it was! I did not feel the joy I had hoped to feel. I knew now what a worthy opponent the whale was.

Even Stubb, when he was done, didn't say a word. He just stood there carefully eyeing the vast corpse he had made.

7 Funeral for a Mighty Creature

The whale Stubb had killed was not Moby Dick. Still, we had done a good job. But our work had just begun. We still had to bring the whale back alongside the ship. There, we would have to cut it up.

There were 18 of us to haul the corpse. We used three small boats. Hour after hour we worked. It seemed to take forever to get that dead body back to the *Pequod*.

Soon it became dark. We were still pulling the dead whale back to the boat. Three lights hung from the *Pequod*. The lights helped guide our way to the ship.

When we finally reached the ship, we could see Ahab. He eyed the whale. He looked a little sad to see that it was not Moby Dick. Ahab gave the order to tie up the whale for the night. Then he went below and we didn't see him again until the next morning.

"A fine greeting," snapped Stubb to himself. "Still, never mind. This is my day, all right." And he laughed. You could never keep Stubb down for long.

Starbuck called out, "Tie up the whale, men. Move!"

We were tired and sore. Yet there was still much to do. All hands went to work. The crew dragged out heavy chains. They pushed them out the portholes.

The chains scraped over the deck and made an awful noise.

We used the heavy chains to tie up the corpse. We tied the head to the stern of the ship and the tail to the bow. The large black body was now as close to the ship as it could be.

"Tomorrow we'll begin to process the whale," said Stubb.

"I can wait," I told him. "I need to sleep for the next week."

Stubb patted me on the back and laughed. "Plenty of time to sleep, lad," he said. "Have some steak with me." Then he turned to cook and called out, "Avast. Sail this way, Cook. Make me a steak."

I thought it was nice of Stubb to offer me a steak. But Queequeg shook his head and said not to eat. It turned out Stubb meant a whale steak! Most sailors don't like to eat it. They say it tastes too fatty. But Stubb loved it. Besides, he had killed the whale. According to tradition, it was his right.

That was fine with me. I had seen enough of that whale's blood. I wanted to forget about it for a while.

I went below deck to try to get some sleep. But no sooner had I nodded off than I heard an awful nose.

"What's that?" I asked Queequeg.

"Sharks," was all he said. And he grabbed his harpoon. He seemed to know what was happening. He went above deck.

Whatever the noise, it was fast and violent. I would not sleep a wink with that going on. So I went above and joined Queequeg to see for myself.

What a sight! Sharks were beginning to eat the whale corpse. They were tearing at the beast's flesh. More blood flowed freely from the whale. The sharks thrashed and flipped. They churned up the red water. Queequeg and Daggoo seemed to know just what to do.

"Put lanterns up over the whale," Queequeg told me. "Put three lanterns out. Light up the water and the whale."

I did as I was ordered. I hung three lanterns on the ship and lit them. The light cast a strange yellow glow over the whale and the red sea.

I could clearly see dozens of sharks attacking the whale corpse. The more blood they drew, the more the sharks came.

"They're eating our whale!" I called out.

"Not for long," said Queequeg.

He and Daggoo grabbed their whale spades and held them up. Whale spades are shaped like garden spades. But they are as sharp as a razor on both sides.

Queequeg and Tashtego leaned over and began striking the attacking sharks. They thrust their whale spades deep into the sharks' skulls.

For hours these two harpooners killed the attacking sharks. Finally the sharks gave up on our whale. They began to feed on themselves. After a time, the ones who were left went away.

What the sharks had failed to do, we would do ourselves. Every sailor became a butcher. We would act like sharks and cut up the dead whale.

The whale had to be cut up so we could take out the oil. We had to use as much of the whale as we could. Then we would store the oil and be on our way. Off to kill another whale.

The next morning I was up and about. I had a new task. I had to help process the whale. And what a task *that* was!

The whale's head was the first part to be removed. Cutting the head is a very difficult job. Whale surgeons pride themselves on their skill. After all, the whale's head is about one-third of its whole body!

Stubb was the surgeon who cut up this whale. Like all whale surgeons, he had to operate about ten feet above the whale. He used long tools. What's more, the whale was still floating in the rough sea while he cut!

Stubb cut many feet deep into the beast. Then he cut through the whale's spinal cord. When the head was cut off, it was tied to the stern and saved. We would have use for it later.

Next, we worked on the body of the whale. A small hole was cut in its side and a hook was placed inside the hole. Next, a deep line was cut into its flesh. Then, with one body and one voice we pulled on a rope. As we pulled, the whale began to roll over and over in the water.

Cutting tackles were shoved in where the line had been cut. As the whale rolled, the blubber began to strip from its body. The blubber clung to the body of the whale like orange rind clings to an orange. And just like an orange rind, the blubber peels off in large strips.

As the blubber was peeled, it was lifted higher and higher out of the water. Then, it just hung there, a bloody mass.

Queequeg picked up what he called a boarding sword. It was a very sharp weapon.

"Stay back," he warned me. He repeated his warning to all the others. Then he lunged at the mass of blubber. He stuck in his sword, once, twice, three times.

Queequeg cut the blubber in two. The upper half was then lowered. We put a fire under it. We melted it down to oil and finally stored this costly liquid in barrels to take home.

Soon the blubber was completely off. We took out the cutting tackles. We removed the giant hooks.

The huge, stripped whale floated away from the ship and back out to sea.

I watched as we moved farther away from the whale. The hungry sharks kept attacking it. Gulls hovered over it. It was a sad funeral for such a mighty creature.

Finally, we had to deal with the head. We hoisted it aloft so we could work on it better near the deck. Remember I told you how skillful Stubb had to be when he cut the head off? There is a very good reason for this.

Inside the head of the sperm whale is a treasure. The whale's head holds as much as 500 gallons of whale oil. If the surgeon is not careful, he could lose this valuable liquid.

Once the head was aloft, Tashtego climbed upon an overhanging yardarm. Then he lowered himself into the head. He began to carefully search for the vat where the oily treasure lay.

Tashtego lowered a bucket inside the skull. Then he raised it up. Inside the bucket was the slimy oil.

It was strange to see the whale's head apart from its body. But there it was, staring up at me, lifeless. I looked into its eyes.

Our eyes are set on the front of our skull. So we see just one image. We focus on one thing only. We see only what's directly in front of us.

The sperm whale's eyes, though, are set on both sides of its head. So it sees two images—one out of each side of the skull. And it sees nothing directly in front.

Odd, I thought. People try to make the world fit their own ideas of right and wrong. They each see things only one way—their way. Too bad we don't see like the whale. We'd get two images instead of one. Maybe then we would see at least two sides to everything.

That was surely Ahab's problem. He could only see Moby Dick in one way—as evil.

Though I had pledged myself to help Ahab hunt Moby Dick down, I could not see whales in only one way. I had helped kill a whale. I helped strip it and bury it at sea. I could not see any whale, even the white whale, as all bad.

Just as I was thinking about Ahab, he came from below deck. He stood beside me, but he paid no attention to me. He just looked at the destroyed whale and shook his head.

I looked into Ahab's eyes. They still burned with a fierce fire. This whale meant nothing to him. His eyes could see only Moby Dick.

8 Ahab and Starbuck's Argument

The crew continued to hunt and kill whales for months. And Captain Ahab continued to think only of killing Moby Dick.

Ahab spent a lot of time below deck. He kept complex charts. He studied the movement of the sperm whales. In this way, he hoped to track down Moby Dick.

When Ahab did come above, he paced. He would pace from bow to stern. Every so often he would pause in his tracks. Then he would stare out to sea.

As time went on, Ahab began to look more and more angry. He was not happy with the whales we had caught. His mind had strayed. He was no longer interested in the business of our whaling adventure. Perhaps he had never been interested. Maybe he had never wanted more than the death of the white whale.

When Ahab was not staring out to sea, he stared at his gold coin. This was the gold coin he'd nailed to the mast and promised to give to the first crewman who spotted Moby Dick.

Ahab studied the coin daily. The coin was nailed into the main mast. The mast had grown old and ragged with age. The nail, too, had grown rusty. But the coin still shone brightly.

It was made of the purest gold. And no crew member dared to touch it. In fact, we felt it was sacred. It was like a good luck charm. It might help us find Moby Dick.

Sometimes Queequeg and I would stand around the mast after our watch. We wondered who might own the coin one day.

"Maybe I'll spy Moby Dick first," I told Queequeg. "I mean, I've had good luck so far."

"Maybe," Queequeg barked. "Queequeg hope you live to spend it."

"Well, that's a fine thought," I said.

"Queequeg no like the feel of this."

"You sound," I said, "like that old prophet Elijah. The one who tried to scare us before we left. Things will be all right," I told him.

As I spoke, I heard a clump-clump sound. I knew right away that it was Ahab. I knew that sound. He always walked that way while the men tried to sleep. What a noise he made!

Queequeg and I watched as Starbuck followed Ahab from below deck. I could see the look on Starbuck's face. He was upset by something. Ahab and Starbuck were in the middle of an argument.

"Listen to me, I tell you," snapped Starbuck.

Ahab would not listen. He just walked away. He

found Queequeg and I looking at the coin. We backed away and let him pass. He ignored us and stared at the gold piece.

"Look at this coin," he said. But he didn't seem to be talking to me or Queequeg. It was as though we did not exist.

Starbuck said, "Many days have I passed that coin. Each man in the crew dreams of one day owning it. But I did not come to you to talk of the coin. The barrels of oil, Captain, are leaking."

But Ahab was in another world. "This coin," he said "shows three mountaintops. Around them is the circle of the world. It shines gold like a little sun. It reflects like a mirror. It shows us our own faces."

Ahab looked at his tiny reflection in the coin. I wondered if he could see the anger in his face. The rage, the hatred! Was it as clear to him as it was to the rest of us? I wondered.

Starbuck brought him back from his dreaming. "I beg of you, Captain, listen. Let go of this white whale for a moment. We have a problem."

"So you said," Ahab snarled. "There be oil in the water. That is nothing to me."

But Starbuck was furious. "Nothing?! We need to get to the problem right away!"

I whispered to Queequeg, "What is the problem?"

Queequeg told me that there must be a leak in one of the barrels of oil below. The crew floods the hold where the barrels are stored. They do this so the wood in the barrels will swell. Then they will have a tight seal. A tight seal keeps the oil in the barrels.

"Then they pump the water out of the hold," said Queequeg. "The water must have been filled with oil. That's how Starbuck knows that there's a leak."

Meanwhile, Starbuck was yelling at Captain Ahab. "We *must* take out all the barrels from the hold. That way we can see which barrel is leaking and fix it."

"It will take too long," Ahab snapped back. "We will be nearing Japan soon. My charts say we are sure to find Moby Dick."

"Sir, if you do not act now, we will lose more oil in one day than we found in a year at sea!" Starbuck cried.

"Begone!" yelled Ahab. "Let the barrels leak. I am not going to sit at anchor for a week to work on a bunch of old wooden barrels."

"What will the owners say?" Starbuck reminded Ahab.

"Hang the owners. I command this ship and I say we push on," Ahab told him. "Now go."

"No," said Starbuck. "We've come twenty thousand miles to get this oil. It's worth saving."

Then Ahab grabbed a pistol from his coat. He pointed it at Starbuck.

Ahab said, "There is one Lord to rule over the

earth. There is one captain to rule over this ship. I
am that lord and master! Out of my sight."

"He's going to kill him!" I said to Queequeg.
Queequeg told me to stay quiet and sit still. I watched
as Starbuck stood eye to eye with Ahab.

Starbuck said to Ahab, "I would tell you to beware
of me. But you would only laugh. Instead, I'll say
this. Beware of yourself, Captain Ahab. You are your
own greatest enemy."

Starbuck started to walk away. Then Ahab said,
"You talk brave enough. But—hah—I see you still
obey me."

Starbuck did not reply. He just continued to walk away. But Ahab already had a different look in his eyes. He was a little calmer now.

Ahab could not help himself. He could hardly control the way he acted. He was a victim of his own hateful desires.

Ahab mumbled, "You think I am my own greatest enemy? Aye, there is some truth to that." He called Starbuck back to his side again.

"You are a good fellow, Starbuck," he told him. Starbuck said nothing. "Order the mates to empty the hold where the barrels rest. Have your look. Find the leak."

And having said that, Ahab went below deck.

"I wonder what made him change his mind?" I whispered to Queequeg.

"He knows deep inside Starbuck is right."

Whatever the reason, Starbuck brought the barrels out of the hold. The crew worked around the clock. We worked hard to find that leaky barrel.

Some of us worked too hard. Queequeg was never able to do things halfway. He put all his strength into the work. He started to grow tired and sick.

"Are you all right?" I asked my friend. But Queequeg was not listening to me.

I turned to look at him. He had the strangest look on his face. It was as though he were staring into the face of death.

"Are you all right?" I repeated. "Queequeg? Should I get the doctor?"

But still Queequeg did not say a word. Then I felt his forehead. It was burning.

"You're on fire," I told him. "I'd better get the doctor double quick. You're like an oven!"

"No," said Queequeg. "Fetch me the carpenter instead."

The carpenter? Had he gone crazy? Had the hard work gotten to him? Had the argument between Starbuck and Ahab upset him so?

"Do as Queequeg say," Queequeg replied. "Fetch the carpenter."

"But why?" I asked him.

The sweat began to stream from his forehead.

"Mr. Starbuck," I called. "Help me get poor Queequeg below." I helped Queequeg to his feet. Starbuck heard my call and came running.

We brought Queequeg to his hammock and laid him out. He rested for a while.

"I got the carpenter for you," I told the sick man. "He'll be along soon. Now why do you want him? Tell me."

Queequeg said that he had once been to a certain port in America. In that port he had seen coffins in the shape of canoes. The whalers from that port were buried in these canoe-like coffins.

Queequeg liked that idea, he told me. The custom was close to that of his own people. When his island people died, they were sent out to sea in a canoe.

Commonly, most sailors are buried in their hammocks. Then, they are left to sink and be eaten by sharks. That is not how Queequeg wanted to go.

"Have him build me canoe. Canoe be my coffin."

"You won't die," I said. "You can't. I won't let you."

Queequeg just smiled and lay still. Soon the carpenter came. He took Queequeg's measurements and built him his coffin.

Into the coffin, Queequeg put some water and a paddle for his trip to the other side.

Then, Queequeg himself got inside. He said he wanted to try it out. He lay there—as still as death. He asked for his little idol Yojo.

Queequeg held Yojo and closed his eyes. I knelt down beside him. "Poor old friend," I cried. "Is it really your time to die?"

It seemed impossible. Queequeg was the strongest man on board. He had risked death a dozen times. He had saved many men from a watery grave. How could he actually be in the arms of death?

"Tell the captain I'm sorry," said Queequeg. "I never got a chance to put my hooks into Moby Dick."

"Never mind that now," I said.

I watched him. A sailor played a tambourine. He seemed to be beating out Queequeg's death march.

9 A Raging Storm

There is a difference between modern people and primitive people. Modern people get very sick and stay sick. They may take six months to get well again. But primitive people can get better in a day.

So it was with Queequeg. As soon as he got all his funeral plans made, he got better. As quickly as he had taken sick, he was just as quickly made whole. No one could understand why.

As for Queequeg, he was very happy. He turned his coffin into a sea chest. He put his clothes and his idol doll Yojo inside. Then he nailed the coffin shut. He sealed it tight. And he never spoke of his sickness again.

Instead, we sang and danced. Pip played his tambourine. Stubb, always merry, sang along. We were all happy to see Queequeg well again.

We sailed on for some time without any sight of Moby Dick. The sea turned choppy. The wind kicked up. Out of the east, clouds rolled in.

East. This was the direction Ahab had bid us sail. This was where he believed Moby Dick would be found. We entered the Japanese seas. Would this area prove to be our watery grave?

The sky began to turn a sickly green and yellow. Black clouds billowed up on the horizon. The wind blew fierce and angry.

Finally, that night, it hit. The worst storm I ever hope to see. Thunder roared and lightning flashed. The *Pequod* was tossed about like a toy boat. A typhoon had hit us. Sheets of water rained down.

The crew rushed on deck. We did our best to hold down the whaling boats. We secured the barrels of oil and the rigging.

Day turned to night. And then the worst of the typhoon came upon us. The rain hit like sharp knives against my face. It ripped apart the sails and tore apart the masts.

The wind tipped the *Pequod* from one side to the other. Waves crashed over the deck. They swept away anything in their path.

"Look up," cried Queequeg as we battled the storm.

I looked up at the masts. Suddenly, I saw the strangest glow in the sky. It was a bright white light. It glowed and pulsed, and danced like fire. The light played about the masts and traveled the length of the deck. It lit up the whole ship.

I remembered seeing such a light before. It was on another one of my voyages. The sailors called it St. Elmo's fire. It is a strange freak of nature. I do not know the cause. But it strikes fear in anyone who sees it.

Sailors are a tough breed. They'll swear up and down. A curse to them is like any other word. But during this weird fire that danced in the sky, all of us were silent. We stood on deck, the rain whipping us. We were lit only by this strange, unearthly light.

Finally Flask spoke to Starbuck. "This can mean no good thing. Please, Starbuck. Tell the captain to turn the ship around."

The rest of the crew began to speak up. Everyone felt this was happening because of Ahab. His sick need to kill his enemy had somehow caused this.

"Turn the ship around," the crew cried.

Then Ahab made his way on deck. The typhoon seemed to mean nothing to him. He looked as he always did—cold and distant. He seemed to think nothing unusual was happening.

"Look up at this fire, men," he cried through the raging storm. "Mark it well. The white flame but leads us to the white whale."

Starbuck yelled back at Ahab. "Turn around. Or we sail to our death." He grabbed Ahab by the arm.

"God is against you," cried Starbuck. "This is a doomed voyage. It began doomed, and we continue doomed. Let me make our way out of this. There is still hope."

But Ahab was not listening. He moved away from Starbuck. Then he threw up his fist and shook it at the fire and light.

"Oh, great fire," shouted Ahab. "Leap! Leap up and lick the sky with your flames. I leap with you. I burn with you. I am one with you. I worship you! You light the way to the white whale. I am not afraid."

"He is mad," I heard Starbuck mutter. And he withdrew his gun. "I could kill him now. If I kill him, we are free."

He took a step closer. Ahab did not notice. The captain was still howling into the storm.

Starbuck said, "We could go home. These sailors could be safe. But do I have it in me to kill him?"

Starbuck brought the gun up higher and aimed. I held my breath. Would he do it? Would Starbuck finally kill Ahab?

I do not know what Starbuck was thinking. I do not know what made him change his mind. Perhaps he knew that killing Ahab would never lift the curse from the *Pequod*. Perhaps he was too good a soul. Murder was not in him. Or it may have been what Ahab shouted next.

He yelled, "Listen to me, men. You all made an oath to hunt the white whale. It is bound up with my oath. And come what may, we will kill Moby Dick. We are all bound together as one. No storm can stop me! And none of you can stop me!"

"Look how he curses the sky," said Stubb. "He has no fear left. He is a madman."

Starbuck put down his gun. He did not shoot Ahab. And the rest of us backed away as well. Ahab had a power it was best not to cross.

The storm continued. Each of us tried our best to save what we could. But Ahab just stood there, unmoved.

He held his face to the sky. He seemed to be daring the lightning to hit him again. Daring the Almighty to give him yet another scar.

I shivered in the cold rain. Giant waves rose up and over the ship. The ghostly glow lit up the sky. And Ahab continued to scream into the wind.

I fell to my knees and prayed to God that He might deliver us from this storm.

10 The *Pequod* Meets the *Rachel*

The next morning the sea was quiet. The sky was clear and the sun shone brightly. A flock of gulls circled above the ship.

Had it all been a dream? A nightmare? No. Here, the masts were split in two. There, the sails were ripped. Everywhere, pieces of rigging littered the deck.

The typhoon had nearly wrecked our ship. We were lucky that we did not lose any men. Slowly the crew went back to work. We cleared up the deck. We mended the sails. We did our best to repair the masts.

But the *Pequod* would never be the same. The storm had taken the life out of the ship.

"Come on, men," said Starbuck. He sounded tired but not beaten. "Let's get this ship a-sailing."

Starbuck was as good a man as I had met. He would not be beat down. Not by man or storm. He knew we had a job to do. We did it. And Starbuck worked as hard as any man.

A few days later Starbuck called out to the crew, "All hands on deck!"

Stubb asked, "What's the problem, mate?"

"A ship is upon us," Starbuck said as he went above deck.

We let out a happy yell. It had been a long time since we had seen another ship.

As I told you before, Ahab did not like these gams. He did not want anything to get in the way of his hunt for Moby Dick. But we hoped *this* gam might be different. Maybe the ship was just out from port. Maybe they carried some news from home. We all raced above deck.

I stood beside Flask and heard him say, "Bad news. She brings bad news."

"How can you tell?" I asked him.

"I can tell," he said.

I thought little of that. Flask was always in a bad mood. But not me. I always hold out hope for the best.

The two ships were nearly side by side now. I could read the name of the visiting ship. She was called the *Rachel.*

Ahab stood by the rail. We knew exactly what he would ask. He asked the same thing every time we came upon another ship.

"Have you seen the white whale?" he asked.

The captain of the *Rachel* cupped his hands and shouted back, "Aye, yesterday."

We all stirred. Ahab himself could barely contain his joy. So we were close to Moby Dick after all!

Then the captain of the *Rachel* asked, "Have you seen a whale boat adrift?"

Ahab replied that he had not seen such a boat. Before Ahab could ask another question, the captain of the *Rachel* came aboard the *Pequod.*

He tried to speak, but Ahab stopped him. Ahab said, "Where is Moby Dick? You didn't kill him, did you? Tell me!"

"No," replied the *Rachel*'s captain.

I could see Ahab breathe a sigh of relief. You would think he'd be happy if Moby Dick was dead. But if you think that, you don't know Ahab. Ahab wanted the white whale for himself.

The captain of the *Rachel* said, "Hear me, Ahab. Yes, we saw the white whale. We sent our boats out to hunt him down. He escaped. But not before he killed some of my crew."

"He is indeed a beast," cried Ahab. "What did I tell you, men? A demon he is."

Then the captain of the *Rachel* said, "One of my men is still missing. So is his whaling boat. I have been searching these waters for him for days. I must find him."

Stubb turned to me and snickered. "Probably someone stole his watch and left with it."

But Starbuck told Stubb to keep quiet. He said no captain wastes the height of the whaling season looking for a thief.

The captain of the *Rachel* grew sad. Tears formed in his eyes. "It's my boy. My son. My own child is among the lost men. I know he is drifting in his boat somewhere in these seas. He is alone. I can almost hear him cry for help! For God's sake, I beg you, Ahab. Help me find my lost son!"

But Ahab stood as cold as stone. "You say you saw this white whale, eh? And that he is still alive."

"Yes," said the other captain. "But my boy—"

"I am sorry for you," said Ahab. "But I have no time for such matters. That whale is close by. If I help you, I stand to lose Moby Dick. I cannot help you. Your son is lost."

I could not believe my ears. None of us could. We had already lost some days searching for the leaky barrels of oil. Surely this was a more important task! What would a few more days matter?

But none of us said a word. We had learned that it was not wise to speak against Ahab.

The other captain said, "I will not go, Ahab, till you say you will help me find my son."

But Ahab ignored him. He called to us: "Men! Be ready to push off. We have work to do!"

The captain of the *Rachel* bowed his head. "Please. Do to me as you would have me do to you," he said.

"Avast!" cried Ahab. "I will not do it. Even now I lose time. Good-bye, sir. God bless you. And may I forgive myself for not helping you. But I must go. Mr. Starbuck! Get a move on. Set a course east. East, I say. Toward Moby Dick. We set sail in three minutes. All hands set to sail!"

"All hands set to sail!" cried Starbuck, and we all jumped into action.

The captain of the *Rachel* moved quietly away. He got back into his boat and his mates rowed him back to his ship.

Soon the two ships went their separate ways. The *Pequod* went to hunt and kill Moby Dick. The *Rachel* set sail to find the captain's lost son.

Poor *Rachel*, I thought. I hoped that the captain would find his son. I watched as the *Rachel* disappeared. The spray foaming at her bow looked like tears.

But had I thought harder, I would have wept for us. I would have wept for the *Pequod*. I could only hope that the *Rachel* would escape what we were about to face.

11 The Final Chase

In the days that passed, the *Pequod* began to look shipshape. The crew had grown happy once more. Ahab spent much of his time below deck. So even the talk of Moby Dick began to fade.

But that's when it all happened. Ahab was on deck. He suddenly whirled around and sniffed the air. He leaned over the railing and then looked to the horizon.

We heard Ahab cry out. "There she blows! There she blows! A hump like a snow hill! It is Moby Dick!"

Now my heart was pounding. Could it really be the white whale? For so long I had lived with the stories of the whale. It was hard to believe he really existed.

"Hah!" said Ahab. "The coin is mine! It was fate that it should fall to me. None of you could find the white whale. I was meant to spot it first!"

I stared out to sea. There it was, indeed. I caught my first sight of Moby Dick! But I had little time to do anything but look. Ahab was in a frenzy.

"Lower the boats, Mr. Starbuck. Lower my boat as well."

"God save us if the captain is right," said Starbuck.

"Is it the white whale?" I asked Queequeg. "Is it really Moby Dick?"

But Queequeg did not reply. He just nodded his head. He looked at me in a strange way, just as he had the day we became good friends. I suddenly remembered all the things we had done, all the adventures we had had. Then, Queequeg put his hand on my shoulder and patted it as if he were saying farewell.

"Ishmael," Starbuck called out. "Avast! And help us lower the boats away."

We lowered the boats. Ahab led the way. My mind was a blank. I stared into the water as I rowed.

The sea was calm—as smooth as glass. The white whale moved quickly away from us. But I could see him clearly now.

There was no doubt about it. This was Moby Dick. This was the beast we had pledged ourselves to hunt. And now we were ready to move in for the kill.

I could see his gleaming white hump. It glided along in a sea of green foam. I could even see the wrinkles on his milky brow.

Sea gulls played above him. He moved along peacefully. He seemed to be having a gentle, joyous swim.

I saw the twisted harpoons still stuck in his flesh. Yet he didn't seem to care about them. It was hard to believe this gentle giant had killed so many men.

"Pull hard, men," shouted Ahab. "We are gaining. Pull hard, I say."

But Moby Dick continued his peaceful swim. The calm tropical sea cradled him. Did he know his hunters were so close?

He might have sensed the dangers. For he suddenly dove deep into the blue waters. We could see his tail rise up out of the water. Then he disappeared.

"He has sounded!" shouted Ahab. "He dives deep. But he will be back. And when he does, we'll be ready for him."

So we waited. The sea remained like glass. The typhoon was no more than a memory now. I gently rocked in Stubb's whale boat. It was like a tropical paradise. Later a sea breeze kicked up and the sea began to swell.

An hour passed. Still no sign of Moby Dick. I thought we had lost him. But Ahab believed we would see him soon.

We continued to wait. Nothing. Ahab leaned over his boat and stared into the water. I did the same.

I could see nothing. What was he looking for? All I could see was my reflection.

But Ahab saw something else. Deep in the water, he saw a small white spot. It had a green glow to it. He continued to stare at it.

The white spot grew bigger. The water remained calm. All at once we saw the white of Moby Dick's brow. Then we saw the whale's huge, gaping mouth. It was rising up from the depths like an open tomb!

The great white whale suddenly broke the surface of the water. Ahab tried to whirl his tiny boat out of the way. But Moby Dick was on top of him.

I heard a horrible crash. Moby Dick had split Ahab's boat in two. His mighty jaw bit into the whaling boat and chopped it to pieces.

Ahab and his crew were thrown from the boat. Moby Dick dove once more. Ahab and his remaining crew thrashed about. But Ahab's peg leg weighed him down.

He went under. Stubb yelled at us to row faster toward him. Starbuck's boat reached Ahab and his crew first.

Starbuck dove in and brought up Ahab. He pulled him aboard his boat. Our boat took in some of the others members of his crew.

Ahab gasped for breath. Starbuck held him. He said, "Oh, Ahab. It's not too late to go back. Leave the white whale alone."

"No!" cried Ahab. "After him. Or he'll destroy us!"

"Sir," Starbuck pleaded. "Moby Dick does not seek you. It's you, *you* who madly seek him. The whale is not the monster. The monster is inside you. Let go before it pulls you down forever."

"Onward, man. You anger me. Do as I say. Stubb. Flask. Starbuck. We seek the whale. Onward!"

And so we followed the white whale as it swam away. We followed Ahab in his madness. I pulled harder than I ever pulled before.

We hunted the white whale another day and night. The three boats were lowered away for the chase. When they once more had the whale in sight, the men hurled their harpoons into him.

Moby Dick fought fiercely. He thrashed about in the seas. His thrashing made the harpoon lines become completely crossed. Before the lines could be cut free, Moby Dick charged the boats. The boats of Stubb and Flask crashed together violently. The boats broke, and the crews were thrown into the sea.

Now Ahab's boat tried to go to their rescue. But Moby Dick smashed his forehead against the boat's bottom. The boat turned over and landed upside down in the water. Ahab and his crew had to struggle out from under it. Moby Dick seemed satisfied with the wreck he had made. He swam off in the opposite direction.

The *Pequod* now dropped a boat and came to the rescue. The ship picked up the stranded seamen, broken oars, and bent harpoon poles. One of the men was lost, and several of them had injured wrists and ankles. And Ahab's ivory leg had snapped. Only one sharp piece of bone was left.

"But no other bones broken, I hope, sir," Stubb said with true concern.

"Even with broken bone, old Ahab is untouched," the captain cried. "No white whale, no man, no devil, can so much as graze old Ahab in his own inner being. You, up there! Which way?"

"Down wind, sir," the lookout replied.

"Pile on the sail again, shipmates!" Ahab cried. "Make the spare boats ready, Mr. Starbuck. Keep him in sight. Ten times I'll circle the world—yes, and dive straight through it—but I'll kill him yet!"

As the sun went down, the whale was still in sight down wind. So once more the sail was shortened for the night. And through the long night hours the sound of hammers could be heard. The weapons were sharpened, and the spare boats were made ready. And the ship's carpenter made Ahab a new leg. Ahab himself stood throughout the night fixed on the quarterdeck, watching for the first sight of the sun.

The morning of the third day dawned fair and fresh. But by noontime the gentle breeze had turned into a gusty wind. The sea grew angry. The waves grew bigger. The spray soaked us all as we pushed forward.

"There she blows," cried Ahab again. "We're upon that beast of a whale!"

God help us, so we were. I could see the whale thrashing in the water. He seemed to be warning us to stay clear. But we did not stay clear. We lowered the boats once more and picked up the chase.

When Ahab's boat got close to the beast, he stood and aimed his harpoon. Then he thrust it into the whale's side. Moby Dick thrashed. He kicked up waves that threw our boats up and out of the water.

Before I knew it, Flask's boat and ours struck each other. I was flung overboard. The two whale boats splintered apart. The crew madly groped about for something to cling to. An oar, a plank, anything!

But the waves were too high now. I saw Flask and Stubb go under. They never came up.

Now Moby Dick turned and moved forward, his giant, crooked jaw leading the charge. He was coming closer and closer.

I saw Queequeg trying to reach for his harpoon. But he fell. Moby Dick was upon him. I saw his giant jaw clasp down upon Queequeg and swallow him whole.

Only Starbuck's boat was left. Once more, Ahab grabbed his harpoon. As the whale passed, he thrust the harpoon into Moby Dick's flesh.

But the rope that held the harpoon to the boat caught Ahab by the neck. And as Moby Dick sped forward, the rope yanked Ahab out of the boat.

Ahab could not free himself. He grasped at the rope in vain. He was being pulled through the water by Moby Dick.

The giant whale spun around. Starbuck's crew dove overboard when they saw the whale approach. But Starbuck just stood at the bow and waited.

Moby Dick smashed into Starbuck's boat. Starbuck was thrown into the sea never to be seen again.

But I could still see Ahab. He had managed to climb atop the whale. He was spearing the great animal over and over again.

"I grow blind! I turn my body from the sun," Ahab shouted. "I give myself over to you. You may destroy everything. But you will not conquer me. I kill you with my hate."

Blood began to spurt from the whale. The sea turned red. As Ahab thrust his spear into Moby Dick, the great beast made a sudden roll. And the rope that had caught Ahab by the neck twisted and snapped. Moby Dick dove once more.

When next the whale surfaced, I could see Ahab's dead body. He was still clutching his harpoon. He was lashed to Moby Dick's body.

I cried out in panic. The whale was headed toward the *Pequod*! He was bearing down on the ship that, even now, was moving toward me to save me. I could not believe my eyes. The beast rammed into the *Pequod* with full force.

Moby Dick's great white brow smashed a giant hole in the ship's side. The water rushed into the ship's hull. The remaining crew scurried about in panic. Some dove to their deaths.

Within seconds, the *Pequod* began to sink. But the whale was not finished. With Ahab still lashed to his side, the whale attacked once more.

Moby Dick rammed full force into the sinking ship. Then he circled the vessel again and again. This circling created wild, swirling water, like water running down a drain. And like water down a drain it carried away everything in its sight.

Moby Dick, Ahab, and the *Pequod* went down, down, down to the very depths of the mighty sea. And suddenly there was silence. The sea was calm once more. I looked around me. "Queequeg!" I cried. "Starbuck! Stubb!" But not a soul answered me. Not a single body but my own was left floating.

I could see nothing. No land, no ships. I was completely alone. The waves rolled by me. They rolled by as they had for five thousand years.

Epilogue

The drama's done. So how can anyone tell this story? Because one survived. One person alone made it through that awful day.

I, Ishmael, survived the last voyage of the *Pequod*. By fate, by God's grace I lived to tell you this tale.

After the *Pequod* went to its watery grave, one piece surfaced. Queequeg's coffin. Days before, he had nailed it shut and sealed it tight. So it floated to the surface with ease.

I swam to that coffin. I held onto it for a day and a night. It was my lifesaver.

I do not know why the sharks left me alone. I cannot tell you why the savage sea hawks did not bother me.

But I can still remember catching sight of a ship on the horizon. I remember thanking God for that ship.

It sailed nearer, nearer, and picked me up at last. That ship was the *Rachel*.

The captain was still searching those waters for his lost son. But he found another lost soul instead. He found me.